A STUDY GUIDE BASED ON THE BOOK

AS SILVER REFINED

KAY ARTHUR

WATERBROOK
PRESS

COLORADO SPRINGS

A Study Guide
to Kay Arthur's As SILVER REFINED
Published by WATERBROOK PRESS
5446 North Academy Boulevard, Suite 200
Colorado Springs, Colorado 80918
A division of Random House, Inc.

Quotations from As *Silver Refined:* © 1997 by Kay Arthur

Scriptures in this book, unless otherwise noted,
are from *The New American Standard Bible* (NASB).
copyright The Lockman Foundation, 1960, 1962, 1963,
1968, 1971, 1973, 1975, 1977.
Used by permission, all rights reserved.

THE REFINER'S FIRE

A companion Bible study to
the introduction, "The Refiner and His Fire,"
and Chapter 1, "When You Feel You're a Failure,"
in AS SILVER REFINED

This image of refinement is something God touches on again and again in His Word. He is the true Refiner. We are His silver.

And the fire is the fire of His making, for through His fire our Refiner will perfect an awesome work, a divine work. He will take what is impure and make it pure. He will take what is dull and make it beautiful. He'll take what is of potential value and reveal its actual value.

He will transform us into treasure....

We want to understand all this well—because the good fire of our loving Refiner is burning. It burns for your good and His glory....

—Kay Arthur in AS SILVER REFINED

---

1. *The Refiner's fire transforms His people into treasure!* In the spaces below, record what you discover in these verses about God's refinement process for His people:

   a. Psalm 66:10-12

b. Isaiah 48:10

c. Daniel 12:10

d. Zechariah 13:9

2. The apostle Peter refers to the refinement of gold while teaching us that trials or testing are a valuable part of the Christian life. Look at 1 Peter 1:6-8. What is the positive result mentioned in verse 7 in connection with the testing of our faith?

3. God uses our trials for our good. Yet our enemy, Satan, seeks the opposite in our lives. Contrast the desires of Satan with the desires of Christ in Luke 22:31-32.

   a. Satan's desire (v.31):

   b. Christ's desire (v.32):

Once you come out of the kingdom of darkness into the kingdom of God, then want it or not it's war—warfare with the prince of this world. And although you can never be snatched from the Father's hand, the devil of darkness will do everything he can to keep you from being an effective witness for our Lord Jesus Christ.

Yes, warfare is inevitable.

—Kay Arthur in AS SILVER REFINED

4. In His Word, God has given us a detailed profile of our enemy. Read the following verses. Using two colors of pencil, pen, or highlighter...
(a) with one color mark every name or description you see in these passages that tells us about the enemy's *character*, what he is *like;*
(b) with the second color, mark everything you see here that tells us about the enemy's *conduct*, what he *does.*

JOHN 8:44
(These are the words Jesus spoke to a group of Jews who had believed in Him in only a superficial way):

You are of your father the devil, and you want to do the desires of your father. He was a murderer from the beginning, and does not stand in the truth, because there is no truth in him. Whenever he speaks a lie, he speaks from his own nature; for he is a liar, and the father of lies.

REVELATION 12:9-10

And the great dragon was thrown down, the serpent of old who is called the devil and Satan, who deceives the whole world; he was thrown down to the earth, and his angels were thrown down with him.

And I heard a loud voice in heaven, saying, "Now the salvation, and the power, and the kingdom of our God and the authority of His Christ have come, for the accuser of our brethren has been thrown down, who accuses them before our God day and night."

a. How would you summarize what you learn in these passages about the enemy's character?

b. How would you summarize what you learn about the enemy's conduct?

5. Satan is a formidable enemy, totally opposed to the will and Word of God. But you are not in the battle alone. Write down the encouragement you find in these verses for the battle:

a. Zechariah 4:6

b. Romans 8:37

c. Philippians 4:13

6. What are the most important things that our "Commander in Chief" tells us in these passages about being a soldier of Christ?

   a. Ephesians 4:27

   b. Ephesians 6:10-18

   c. 2 Timothy 2:3-4

   d. 1 Peter 5:8-9

In this study we'll focus primarily on understanding and overcoming the strategies of Satan that begin with our *disappointment*. Together these attacks from the enemy make up a dangerous spiral that we can call the Five Deadly D's:

The downward spiral begins...with disappointment. Disappointment comes when our expectations aren't met. Consequently we're not happy about it—we're disturbed.

When this happens and we don't conquer that disappointment in God's way, then we spin downward into *discouragement*. We're without courage. We want to give up. We want to quit because we're disheartened. We're ready to run rather than deal with the situation. Isn't this evident today as we see many who, in the face of adversities, name the name of Christ while throwing up their hands or shoving them into their pockets? They walk out; they run away. Their fighting spirit—their spunk—is gone.

And what follows discouragement? Depression in its various degrees.

The first "degree" of depression is *dejection*—a lowness of spirit, a feeling of spiritual and emotional fatigue.

If not reversed this dejection takes us down even further, plunging us into despair and finally into utter demoralization. At this stage of descent, hope is entirely abandoned and is replaced by apathy and numbness. Fear becomes overwhelming and paralyzing and can degenerate further into disorder and reckless action that is heedless of consequences.

—Kay Arthur in *AS SILVER REFINED*

7. Pause and reflect on the last time you recall having encountered a major disappointment.

a. How did you handle it?

b. Where did it lead?

The front line is always the mind. Never forget that principle, for understanding it is the key to winning the war…. Your mind is all-important….

Do you realize that *how you think* really determines how you behave?…

> Satan chooses the mind for his battleground because he understands so well the principle laid down in the Word, that as a man thinketh so he is....
>
> —Kay Arthur in *As Silver Refined*

8. Read 2 Corinthians 10:3-5.

  a. Study verses 3 and 4. What is true *negatively* about our "weapons"? What are they *not* like?

  b. And what is true *positively* about our weapons? What is their nature, and what can they do?

  c. According to verse 5, what is it that Paul says is to be demolished or destroyed?

  d. In accomplishing this, what are we to do in our minds?

  e. What kinds of harmful thoughts does the enemy often use to attack your own mind?

9. Another key passage regarding our minds is Romans 12:1-2.

   a. What are we specifically commanded to do in verse 2?

   b. Write down any ideas about how you might better obey this command.

10. What should you be concentrating your thoughts on, according to these verses?

    a. Philippians 4:8

    b. Colossians 3:2

    c. In a typical day for you, what are the most practical and effective ways in which you can follow the standards and commands given to us for our thought life in Philippians 4:8 and Colossians 3:2?

11. Think of an area of your life where you have been defeated by Satan in the past. What have you learned

from this study that you can put into action the next time he attempts to test you?

_____

> My goal is that no matter how fierce or long the battles we face, you and I together will be able to say, "But in all these things we overwhelmingly conquer through Him who loved us" (Romans 8:37).
>
> —Kay Arthur in *AS SILVER REFINED*

_____

12. In all the selections quoted in this lesson from *As Silver Refined,* underline the points that have the most personal significance for you.

13. Carefully write out **James 1:2-4** in the space below, then begin committing this passage to memory.

In time alone with God, review what you have written down and learned in this lesson. Then pray for the Lord's strength to overcome in any battles you are presently experiencing. Record here any further thoughts or prayer requests that come to your mind and heart.

FACING
DISAPPOINTMENT—
PART I

*A companion Bible study
to Chapter 2, "God's Training in Disguise,"
in As Silver Refined*

Disappointment—it comes whenever expectations aren't
fulfilled, whenever you and I are left wanting. Hopes are
unreached, desires unmet. To be disappointed is to be
unsatisfied or displeased with some situation or person—
or with ourselves or even with God....

Your disappointment is like an overhanging cloud
separating you from the warmth of the Son. A chill comes
over you, and you shudder. Drawing your arms tighter
around yourself doesn't help. You ache but not with
physical pain. You find it hard to concentrate, hard to
listen to what others are saying. All you can think of is the
disappointment intruding into your world.

—Kay Arthur in AS SILVER REFINED

---

1. Read through all the selections quoted in this lesson
   from *As Silver Refined,* and underline the points that
   have the most personal significance for you.

2. Look closely at Jesus' statements in John 16:33, which contain words of warning, encouragement, and promise.

   a. *Why* did Jesus say He was speaking these words to them? What was His purpose?

   b. Now look at the words of warning, encouragement, and promise in the middle and last parts of the verse. How exactly do you think knowing these things would help us accomplish the purpose Jesus stated at the beginning of the verse?

   c. How would you describe the personal encouragement that you draw from these words?

Because we are His and He is ours, we can take courage. We must take courage.

   "But *how?*" you ask. That, beloved, is what this book is all about— to help you with the *how*…and to give you a glimpse into the *why*…and to make you aware of the awful pit of despair you can fall into if you do not handle life's disappointments God's way.

—Kay Arthur in *As Silver Refined*

---

3. In the following verses...
   (a) circle the important words that are used more than once in this passage;
   (b) underline or highlight the *commands* in this passage—what we're specifically told to do;
   (c) and mark in another color the *effects* or *results* that we're to be aware of.

JAMES 1:2-4

Consider it all joy, my brethren, when you encounter various trials, knowing that the testing of your faith produces endurance. And let endurance have its perfect result, that you may be perfect and complete, lacking in nothing.

a. Look again at the last sentence in the verse. In your own words, write what kind of character attributes you expect to see manifested in your life as you grow toward this "perfection" and "completion." Envision your maturity, and describe it as fully as you can here.

b. Why do you think God wants us to know that the testing of our faith produces endurance?

Remember again with me, won't you, our lesson in battle strategy: The best way to win is to respond rightly to the enemy's first penetrating attack. It's critical that in the battlefield of your mind you know how to handle disappointments before you find yourself slipping or even spiraling downward into the Deadly D's. If you fail to handle a disappointment biblically and quickly, you open yourself up to the enemy, making yourself a bigger target. You allow the enemy to infiltrate your mind and begin building a stronghold inside you brick by brick, and *he will snare you from within.*

Your first response, my friend, must be an act of pure obedience.... Determine by faith that you will simply change the "D" of disappointment to an "H," then add a space—and you'll eventually see that this really is *His appointment....*

What does it mean—practically—to change disappointment to His appointment?...

No matter what happens, beloved, no matter how disappointing it is, you must first, in an act of the will, *rejoice and pray and give thanks.*

—Kay Arthur in *AS SILVER REFINED*

4. The following passages are ones that Kay Arthur refers to as "aspirin to relieve the ache" when we encounter disappointment.
(a) Circle in a bright color any word or phrase in these passages that has to do with joy.
(b) In another color, underline or highlight the *commands* in this passage—what we're specifically told to do (or not to do).
(c) In a third color, mark the foundational truths that we are to know and understand as the background for our obedience.

ROMANS 5:3-5; EPHESIANS 5:18-20;
AND 1 THESSALONIANS 5:16-18

And not only this, but we also exult in our tribulations, knowing that tribulation brings about perseverance; and perseverance, proven character; and proven character, hope; and hope does not disappoint, because the love of God has been poured out within our hearts through the Holy Spirit who was given to us.

And do not get drunk with wine, for that is dissipation, but be filled with the Spirit, speaking to one another in psalms and hymns and spiritual songs, singing and making melody with your heart to the Lord; always giving thanks for all things in the name of our Lord Jesus Christ to God, even the Father...

Rejoice always; pray without ceasing; in everything give thanks; for this is God's will for you in Christ Jesus.

a. What aspects of obeying these verses are hardest for you personally?

b. What do you believe are the most important keys to obeying these commands promptly when you face disappointments?

5. Look at Paul's "even if" statement in Philippians 2:17. Then write your own personal version of this verse. Envision and express before God your desire "to rejoice and to share my joy with others, *even if*—" (then complete that sentence with the kinds of disappointments and trials you want to have victory over).

Just watch what God does when you truly trust Him and walk by faith rather than by sight or by feelings.

—Kay Arthur in *AS SILVER REFINED*

---

6. Look at Paul's words in Philippians 1:12-14, written while he was imprisoned in Rome for preaching the gospel. How did God use his circumstances to impact...

   a. his captors?

   b. his comrades?

7. Carefully consider the dynamic truths in each of the following passages, then respond by stating how each one can help you personally to walk by faith and not by sight.

   a. Psalm 22:3-5

b. Isaiah 50:10

c. 2 Corinthians 5:7   .

d. Colossians 2:6

8. Look at the instruction given to us in 1 Peter 4:12.
   How can you apply this verse to your life today?

It falls back on this: *What do you really know about God?*
Everything falls back on that—our trust, our faith, our
obedience. And how do we get to know God so that *we
know that we know?*

Only through His Word....

Being in God's Word and knowing it *for yourself* is the
key.

If you tithed the hours of each day, you would owe
God two hours and twenty-four minutes *a day.* How
much time are you giving to knowing Him and to
having fellowship with Him? How much time are you
spending in His Word, the Word that is the very bread
by which we live?

—Kay Arthur in *AS SILVER REFINED*

---

9. What is your current plan and practice for Scripture intake in each of the following categories?

   a. Bible reading:

   b. Bible study:

   c. Bible memorization:

   d. Hearing messages and sermons from Bible teachers:

   e. Scripture meditation:

The disappointment has come, precious child of God, not because God desires to hurt you or make you miserable or to demoralize you or ruin your life or keep you from ever knowing happiness. Rather, it comes because He wants you to be perfect and complete in every aspect, lacking nothing. When you see your Father face to face, He doesn't want you to be ashamed or sorry....

It's not the easy times that make you more like Jesus but the hard times. So don't be surprised that God permits crushing disappointments in your life; instead, keep on rejoicing....

I wouldn't trade this for anything. Can you and I always say that about our disappointments?

—Kay Arthur in *As Silver Refined*

---

10. For helpful review, write out **James 1:2-4** from memory in the space below.

Perhaps there's a difficult situation in your life now in which you haven't changed the *D* of disappointment into an *H*. In time alone with God, review what you have written down and learned in this lesson, and bring before Him this disappointing situation.

As Kay Arthur says, "Pause right now… putting your feelings and your desire and commitment into a prayer to your heavenly Father. Say to Him, 'I don't understand it all, Father, but I will believe that this is Your appointment. Your Word says that You are sovereign, and You must have a purpose in this. Therefore I choose to believe it. I rest in You.'"

Record here the thoughts or prayer requests that come to your heart and mind from this time with God.

∾

FACING DISAPPOINTMENT— PART 2

A companion Bible study to Chapter 3,
"Present Failures, Past Regrets," in As Silver Refined

When I say that your every disappointment can become *His* appointment to make you more like Jesus, do you wonder, *Even if I fail?...Even if I sin?*

Yes, beloved, even if you sin, even if you fail. And though you can't get away with using this as an excuse to sin or fall, if you're truly His child, you can know that when you do sin God will teach you a lesson through it and use it to change you more into His likeness.

—Kay Arthur in *AS SILVER REFINED*

---

1. Summarize here the most important truths you have learned so far in this book about dealing with disappointment.

2. Read through all the selections quoted in this lesson from *As Silver Refined,* and underline the points that have the most personal significance for you.

3. Think carefully about Hebrews 12:5-7 and 12:11-13.

   a. From these verses, how do you see and understand that God's discipline is positive, healthy, and constructive for us?

   b. In what specific ways has God used your present or past failures to accomplish positive discipline in your life?

When it comes to dealing with failure, know this: You're not alone.... If we're honest we all admit to dealing with tendencies toward defeat, depression, and even the despair that failure can bring when it isn't dealt with in a biblical way.

—Kay Arthur in *As Silver Refined*

---

4. Think of a particular area of recent or current personal failure in your life.

   a. Write down just enough words here to identify this failure for your own recall.

   b. In your own estimation, what were all the causes of this failure?

5. *Getting God's perspective:* Think again about the area of personal failure that you identified in the previous question. In the space below, describe as fully as you can how you think the basic truths in each of the following verses relate to this failure. *(Think personally!)*

a. Psalm 73:26

b. Romans 3:23

c. Hebrews 12:1

d. 1 John 1:9

e. Jude 24-25

To fail is to be humbled. Failure makes us aware of our own impotence, our imperfections, our shortcomings. Failure brings us low. If we respond properly by humbling ourselves before our heavenly Father, then according to James 4:10 we'll find Him exalting us. And when God exalts us after we experience the humiliation and defeat of failing, then it's a safe exaltation rather than a source of pride that eventually leads only to greater defeat and failure....

Failure can be either a stumbling block that flattens you or a steppingstone to a life of success built upon the immovable Cornerstone. It's all a matter of whom you choose to believe....

God and obedience to His precepts are what take us from failure to success by humbling us to the point where we know the only way to genuinely succeed—to be blameless—is *through Him*.

—Kay Arthur in AS SILVER REFINED

6. How do you think your present and past failures can help you to *better* obey the commands mentioned in these verses? (Be as specific as you can.)

   a. Romans 12:3

   b. James 4:10

The first thing you must *not* do is to think there's no hope, no help, no way out. That would be to deny the power of the One who rescued you from the greatest of all failures or to deny the fact that God is *for* you.

—Kay Arthur in AS SILVER REFINED

7. Sometimes specific sins on our part are at the root of the failure and regret we experience. Look at David's example of confession in the verses below from Psalm 51.
   (a) Underline or highlight in one color the key words and phrases that show what David asks God to do with

his sin and sinful condition.

(b) Mark with a second color key words and phrases that show what David anticipates as the results in his life of God's cleansing.

PSALM 51 (SELECTED VERSES)

[1] Be gracious to me, O God, according to Thy lovingkindness; according to the greatness of Thy compassion blot out my transgressions.

[2] Wash me thoroughly from my iniquity, and cleanse me from my sin.

[7] Purify me with hyssop, and I shall be clean; wash me, and I shall be whiter than snow.

[10] Create in me a clean heart, O God, and renew a steadfast spirit within me.

[11] Do not cast me away from Thy presence, and do not take Thy Holy Spirit from me.

[12] Restore to me the joy of Thy salvation, and sustain me with a willing spirit.

[13] Then I will teach transgressors Thy ways, and sinners will be converted to Thee.

[14] Deliver me from bloodguiltiness, O God, Thou God of my salvation; then my tongue will joyfully sing of Thy righteousness.

[15] O Lord, open my lips, that my mouth may declare Thy praise.

a. What important truths do these verses from Psalm 51 indicate about God's character, as David understands it?

b. What do you think are the most important requests in this psalm for us to know and use after our own times of personal sin?

8. What personal encouragement do you find in the following glimpses of God's character? (Express it in your own words of gratitude.)

a. Psalm 103:12

b. Lamentations 3:22-23

c. Hebrews 10:15-17

Whatever happened, happened. We can't remake our past.
But with God we can handle the past. With God,
whatever has happened in the past need not destroy us....

No matter what has happened in our backgrounds, with God there is grace, peace, and hope if we'll run to Him and bring every past disappointment captive to faith in His Word....

Even the negative consequences we face from our past are part of the "all things" God uses to work together for our good.

—Kay Arthur in AS SILVER REFINED

9. Look in Isaiah 43:18-19 at God's words to His people Israel.

a. What did God tell them to do regarding the past?

b. What did He instead focus their attention on, and with what promises did He do this?

10. From what you see in 1 Timothy 1:12-15, how would you summarize how Paul overcame any regret he might have had about his past?

11. Think of a particular aspect of your past over which you recently or currently have experienced regret. Write down just enough words here to identify what it is in your past that brought on this regret.

12. *Getting God's perspective:* Think again about the area of past regret that you identified in the previous question. In the space below, describe as fully as you can how you think the basic truths in each of the following verses relate to this regret. *(Think personally!)*

   a. Philippians 3:13-14

   b. 2 Corinthians 5:17

   c. Psalm 40:1-3

13. Follow this counsel from Kay Arthur: "Take a few minutes now to think about these negatives from your past that linger in your thoughts and concerns. What positive changes have they brought about in your own character and in your relationship with God and with others?"

14. For helpful review, write out **James 1:2-4** from memory.

In time alone with God—who through the life and words of His Son Jesus Christ has shown us that He is meek and humble in heart (Matthew 11:29)—review what you have written down and learned in this lesson. Then record here any personal prayer requests that come to your heart and mind.

LEARNING MEEKNESS— PART I

A companion Bible study to Chapter 4,
"Facing the Stress," in As Silver Refined

There'll always be tension to life. Yet it needs to be a healthy, creative tension, not life-sapping stress. Few of us can truly cope well with unrelenting stress. It's destructive. Our society bears witness to that. It's more than people can take....

I believe a major cause for this stress is that we react rather than act.

—Kay Arthur in AS SILVER REFINED

---

1. Read through all the selections quoted in this lesson from *As Silver Refined*, and underline the points that have the most personal significance for you.

2. In our battle with stress, what specific *actions*—rather than *reactions*—are taught in Philippians 4:6-7?

3. From what you see in John 14:27, how much stress (and what kinds) does Jesus expect His followers to experience?

God knows what each one of us is dealing with. He knows our pressures. He knows our conflicts. And He has made provision for each and every one of them. That provision is Himself in the person of the Holy Spirit, indwelling us and empowering us to *respond rightly*....

No matter what happens to us, God has totally and completely and absolutely equipped and prepared us for it.

So I'm not to fight these afflictions I encounter, the trials and disappointments, these oppressions, these humbling situations. God is in perfect control of them, and in His perfect design He's permitted them to teach me to act rather than react. He has me in training.

—Kay Arthur in *As Silver Refined*

4. In facing stress, and the trials and temptations that so readily come with it, what encouragement do you find in 1 Corinthians 10:13? (Express this in your own words.)

5. Look at the great truths in these verses about God's provision for us. Summarize in your own words what each one means for us in learning meekness as we face daily stress.

   a. Romans 8:26-27

   b. Romans 8:34

c. Hebrews 4:15

d. Philippians 4:13

6. Write your personal responses below to these questions and suggestions from Kay Arthur: "So what will you do if someone cuts you down in public? Have you thought about that? What will you do if someone you love discredits you in front of people? If you're wrongly accused, will you act or react? How will you respond if members of your family turn against you and your commitment to Christ? Will you remember that God is your defender? These are circumstances to consider right now and determine that you'll respond in meekness, so that when they come, the Spirit of God will be quick to remind you of your commitment."

Meekness is the key to *acting* rather than *reacting* when disappointments come....

God is at work to build meekness into our innermost beings. And the way He works meekness into our characters is through disappointments and trials....

*Meekness is born in stress, in trials, in affliction, in
conflict...in difficulties.* Meekness is born in situations that
humble you.

—Kay Arthur in *As Silver Refined*

---

7. Read the following words spoken by Moses to the
people of Israel.
(a) Mark in one color the key words and phrases that
tell *what* it is that God did to His people.
(b) With a second color, mark the key words and
phrases that indicate *why* God did this.

DEUTERONOMY 8:2-3

And you shall remember all the way which the Lord your
God has led you in the wilderness these forty years, that
He might humble you, testing you, to know what was in
your heart, whether you would keep His commandments
or not.

And He humbled you and let you be hungry, and fed
you with manna which you did not know, nor did your
fathers know, that He might make you understand that
man does not live by bread alone, but man lives by
everything that proceeds out of the mouth of the Lord.

a. In what way have you seen God doing this same
thing in your life?

b. What would you say are the most important truths this passage teaches us about the character of the Lord our God?

8. *Reason for praise:* According to Psalm 25:8-10, what is it about God that causes Him to teach and guide the humble?

9. What truths do these passages teach that help make meekness easier for us when facing unjust treatment from other people?

   a. Deuteronomy 32:41

   b. Romans 12:19

   c. 2 Thessalonians 1:6-8

10. Review what God's Word says about *pride*—which is opposite from meekness—in these verses:

a. Proverbs 3:34

b. Proverbs 8:13

c. Proverbs 16:18

d. Proverbs 29:23

e. Isaiah 13:11

When it comes to learning about meekness, we have the perfect Teacher....

"Although He was a Son, *He learned obedience from the things which He suffered*" (Hebrews 5:8). In whatever things we are suffering—are we learning obedience?

—Kay Arthur in *AS SILVER REFINED*

---

11. Read the following verses (all of which include words spoken by Jesus) from the Gospel of John.
(a) In one color, mark a triangle on or above every name or pronoun that refers to God the Father.
(b) In a second color, mark a cross on or above every name or pronoun that refers to Jesus.

5:19 Truly, truly, I say to you, the Son can do nothing of Himself, unless it is something He sees the Father doing; for whatever the Father does, these things the Son also does in like manner.

8:28-29 When you lift up the Son of Man, then you will know that I am He, and I do nothing on My own initiative, but I speak these things as the Father taught Me. And He who sent Me is with Me; He has not left Me alone, for I always do the things that are pleasing to Him.

8:38 I speak the things which I have seen with My Father....

12:49-50 For I did not speak on My own initiative, but the Father Himself who sent Me has given Me commandment, what to say, and what to speak. And I know that His commandment is eternal life; therefore the things I speak, I speak just as the Father has told Me.

14:10 Do you not believe that I am in the Father, and the Father is in Me? The words that I say to you I do not speak on My own initiative, but the Father abiding in Me does His works.

14:31 ...but that the world may know that I love the Father, and as the Father gave Me commandment, even so I do....

a. Focusing on Christ's example as you see it in these passages, how would you summarize His meekness before God the Father?

b. Look closely again at what these passages say about how Jesus depended on God the Father. How would you express these same principles as they apply personally to you?

12. Carefully write out **Matthew 11:28-30** in the space below, then begin committing this passage to memory.

In time alone with God, review what you have written down and learned in this lesson. Record here any personal prayer requests that come to your heart and mind.

LEARNING MEEKNESS— PART 2

A companion Bible study to Chapter 5,
"Transformed Under His Control,"
in As Silver Refined

First of all, meekness isn't natural.... Meekness is something God works into us. It isn't a personality temperament but a fruit of the Holy Spirit.... If you're a believer, your genetic structure spiritually is all there for meekness. You only have to walk in it, participate in it....

To be meek is to be calmly strong. Meekness is supernatural. It's an inwrought grace of the soul.

—Kay Arthur in *AS SILVER REFINED*

---

1. In the selections quoted in this lesson from *As Silver Refined,* underline the points that have the most personal significance for you.

2. Psalm 37 is in many ways an Old Testament portrait of meekness.
   (a) Mark in one color every command that is given to us in this passage.
   (b) With a second color, mark every result that is promised to those who heed these words.

PSALM 37 (SELECTED VERSES)

[1] Do not fret because of evildoers, be not envious toward wrongdoers.

[2] For they will wither quickly like the grass, and fade like the green herb.

[3] Trust in the LORD, and do good; dwell in the land and cultivate faithfulness.

[4] Delight yourself in the LORD; and He will give you the desires of your heart.

[5] Commit your way to the LORD, trust also in Him, and He will do it.

[6] And He will bring forth your righteousness as the light, and your judgment as the noonday.

[7] Rest in the LORD and wait patiently for Him; do not fret because of him who prospers in his way, because of the man who carries out wicked schemes.

[8] Cease from anger, and forsake wrath; do not fret, it leads only to evildoing.

[9] For evildoers will be cut off, but those who wait for the LORD, they will inherit the land.

[10] Yet a little while and the wicked man will be no more; and you will look carefully for his place, and he will not be there.

[11] But the humble [the meek] will inherit the land, and will delight themselves in abundant prosperity....

[27] Depart from evil, and do good, so you will abide forever.

²⁸ For the LORD loves justice, and does not forsake His godly ones; they are preserved forever; but the descendants of the wicked will be cut off.

²⁹ The righteous will inherit the land, and dwell in it forever....

³⁴ Wait for the LORD, and keep His way, and He will exalt you to inherit the land; when the wicked are cut off, you will see it....

³⁹ But the salvation of the righteous is from the LORD; He is their strength in time of trouble.

⁴⁰ And the LORD helps them, and delivers them; He delivers them from the wicked, and saves them, because they take refuge in Him.

a. Which of these commands is the hardest for you to follow as a pattern of meekness in your life right now?

b. From what you see taught here in Psalm 37, what would you say are the most important attributes of the meek and righteous person?

c. What *promises* in this psalm are the most appealing to you personally at this time?

3. In light of what you've learned from Psalm 37, how would you explain the meaning of Jesus' words in Matthew 5:5?

4. How would you also explain the meaning of 1 Peter 5:6?

In every situation, in any and all things, meekness is able to remember the meekness of Christ and to give thanks and to praise God.

—Kay Arthur in *As Silver Refined*

---

5. What do you think is most significant about the portrait of Jesus Christ given in Matthew 21:5?

6. Look in Isaiah 66:2 at all the description of the person whom God esteems.

   a. In what ways does this description fit Jesus Christ in His earthly life?

   b. In what ways does it fit you?

> Why should I ever resist any delay or disappointment,
> any affliction or oppression or humiliation—when I
> know God will use it in my life to make me like Jesus and
> to prepare me for heaven?
>
> —Kay Arthur in *As Silver Refined*

7. What impresses you most about David's example of meekness in 2 Samuel 16:9-13?

8. In your own words, give written thanks to God for what you see in these verses about His regard for the humble.

   a. Psalm 147:6

   b. Psalm 149:4

9. For helpful review, write out **Matthew 11:28-30** from memory.

In time alone with the Lord, review what you have written down and learned in this lesson. Then list here any personal prayer requests that come to your heart and mind, as well as any commitments you want to express to God—who Himself guides the meek and humble and teaches them His way, and sustains them, and crowns them with salvation (Psalm 25:9, 147:6, 149:4).

LESSON SIX

LEARNING MEEKNESS—
PART 3

A companion Bible study to Chapter 6,
"Strength in the Face of Stresses," in As Silver Refined

Meekness means you're in control—in the Spirit's control.
You don't let the situation alter who you are or determine
how you respond.

In meekness you acknowledge that affliction or
oppression or humbling situations have come your way as
situations permitted by God, yet you still do not let them
rule over you.

—Kay Arthur in AS SILVER REFINED

---

1. Summarize here the most important truths you've
   studied in the past two lessons about living in
   meekness.

2. In the selections quoted in this lesson from *As Silver
   Refined,* underline the points that have the most
   personal significance for you.

3. In each of the following verses, the Greek word *prautes* ("meekness") is used. In some English versions it is also translated as "gentleness" or "humility."
   (a) In each passage, circle the word meekness.
   (b) With a second color, mark every key word or phrase that indicates the *action* in our lives that is to be associated with meekness.

   EPHESIANS 4:1-2, COLOSSIANS 3:12,
   JAMES 1:21; AND JAMES 3:13 (NKJV)

   I, therefore, the prisoner of the Lord, entreat you to walk in a manner worthy of the calling with which you have been called, with all humility and gentleness [meekness], with patience, showing forbearance to one another in love....

   And so, as those who have been chosen of God, holy and beloved, put on a heart of compassion, kindness, humility, gentleness [meekness] and patience....

   Therefore putting aside all filthiness and all that remains of wickedness, in humility [meekness] receive the word implanted, which is able to save your souls....

   Who is wise and understanding among you? Let him show by good conduct that his works are done in the meekness of wisdom.

4. Read over the incident involving Moses, Aaron, and Miriam as related in Numbers 12. Summarize in your own words the action that takes place in each part of this chapter:

a. 12:1-3

b. 12:4-9

c. 12:10-13

d. 12:14-16

5. Compare what we learn about Moses in Numbers 12:3 with what God says about him in 12:6-8. From this comparison, what conclusions can you make about God's definition of meekness (or humility)?

6. Read what the godly man Stephen said about Moses in Acts 7:20-40. What conclusions about the meekness of Moses can you draw from this passage?

7. From each of the following passages, what conclusions can you draw about the meekness of Jesus, our Teacher of meekness?

    a. John 2:12-17

b. Matthew 21:23-27

c. Matthew 22:15-22

d. Matthew 23:27-33

e. Matthew 26:6-13

f. Matthew 26:36-44

It is the meek who believe that God is everything, and
they live accordingly.

—Kay Arthur in *AS SILVER REFINED*

---

8. Look at the words of the Song of Moses in
   Deuteronomy 32:3-4. How did Moses demonstrate his
   belief that "God is everything"?

9. What does it mean to you personally that "God is
   everything"? Express this in your own words, in the
   form of praise to God.

10. In James 4, notice the three commands given to us in verses 6, 7, and the first half of verse 8. List these commands here, in their correct order.

When there's true meekness toward God, then there also can be and must be true meekness toward other people.

—Kay Arthur in *AS SILVER REFINED*

---

11. *For your own life,* what practical expressions and examples of meekness toward other people do you see in these passages?

   a. Matthew 25:34-40

   b. Romans 13:1

   c. Romans 14:1,13

   d. Ephesians 5:21-25

   e. Ephesians 6:1-5

f. Hebrews 13:17

12. Look again at the practical arenas of meekness which you wrote about in the previous question.

    a. In which of these areas do you think God would like to see more improvement in your own life?

    b. If by His grace and power that improvement was made, what would be different about your life?

13. For helpful review, write out **Matthew 11:28-30** from memory.

In time alone with our God—who truly is everything— review what you have written down and learned in this lesson. Record here any personal prayer requests that come to your heart and mind, as well as any commitments you want to express to Him.

BELIEVING GOD'S SOVEREIGNTY—PART 1

A companion Bible study to Chapter 7,
"Facing the Pain," in As Silver Refined

I know the topic of God's sovereignty can seem so heavy—especially if you don't study God's Word on your own and if you believe only what you've been taught from the Word by someone else. But take what I am saying and test it with what you read through the whole Word of God. If it meets the test then live by it, and you'll know how to handle every disappointment, no matter how painful.

—Kay Arthur in *AS SILVER REFINED*

---

1. In the selections quoted in this lesson from *As Silver Refined,* underline the points that have the most personal significance for you.

2. What do each of these passages teach us about the sovereignty of God?

   a. Psalm 103:19

   b. Isaiah 14:24

3. Jeremiah 29 records the text of a letter which the prophet Jeremiah wrote to the Jewish exiles in Babylon, following the devastating Babylonian attack upon Jerusalem.

   a. Summarize what Jeremiah told the people to do in verses 4-7.

   b. What foundational promise from God does Jeremiah pass on to the exiles in Babylon in verse 10?

   c. What positive truth from God does Jeremiah pass on to the exiles in Babylon in verse 11?

   d. What were the promises of God associated with this positive truth, as they are detailed in verses 12-14?

   e. How would you summarize what this passage teaches us about the character of God, and about the sovereignty of God?

Life is fraught not only with stress and tense relationships and everyday disappointments but also with acute, piercing pain....If you're going to respond to this inescapable pain in meekness...then you have to know two things:

You have to realize that God is in control, that He is sovereign.

And you have to understand who He is. You have to know God's heart, His character, His attributes.

And when the pain is deepest and sharpest—engulfing the world around us and infiltrating our own hearts and lives as well—it becomes a testing and proving ground both for our belief in the sovereignty of God and for our understanding of His heart.

—Kay Arthur in *AS SILVER REFINED*

4. Read in Daniel 4 about the lesson on God's sovereignty that King Nebuchadnezzar of Babylon learned the hard way.

   a. In verses 1-3, what summary statements about God does Nebuchadnezzar make as he begins telling his story?

   b. Summarize the action that takes place in verses 4-8.

   c. Summarize Nebuchadnezzar's dream, as he relates it in verses 9-18.

d. Summarize Daniel's interpretation of the dream, from verses 19-26.

e. What advice does Daniel give in verse 27?

f. Summarize the action that takes place in verses 28-33.

g. What important conclusions does Nebuchadnezzar make about his experience in verses 34-37?

h. How would you summarize the most important lessons we can learn from this passage about the sovereignty of God?

> The single most powerful, liberating, peace-giving truth
> I've ever learned in God's Word is the fact that He is
> sovereign. It has been a mainstay in my life.
>
> —*Kay Arthur in As Silver Refined*

5. Read the following verses from throughout Scripture.
   (a) Mark a triangle on or above every name or pronoun
   for God.
   (b) With a second color, mark every key word or
   phrase that indicates what God does or has done in His
   sovereignty.

DEUTERONOMY 32:39; PSALM 103:19; ISAIAH 14:24,27 AND 45:5-7; AND EPHESIANS 1:11-12

"See now that I, I am He, and there is no god besides me;
it is I who put to death and give life. I have wounded, and
it is I who heal; and there is no one who can deliver from
My hand...."

The LORD has established His throne in the heavens;
and His sovereignty rules over all....

The LORD of hosts has sworn saying, "Surely, just as I
have intended so it has happened, and just as I have
planned so it will stand.... For the LORD of hosts has
planned, and who can frustrate it? And as for His
stretched-out hand, who can turn it back?..."

"I am the LORD, and there is no other; besides me
there is no God....that men may know from the rising to
the setting of the sun that there is no one besides me. I

am the LORD, and there is no other, the One forming light and creating darkness, causing well-being and creating calamity; I am the LORD who does all these...."

In Him also we have obtained an inheritance, having been predestined according to His purpose who works all things after the counsel of His will, to the end that we who were the first to hope in Christ should be to the praise of His glory.

a. What do you believe are the strongest truths that these passages together teach us about God's sovereignty?

b. In what ways, if any, does knowing these truths give you peace and a sense of freedom?

God, and *only* God, is able to be sovereign.... Only God is in charge, and if you and I understand this, we can bow the knee before Him....

God is in charge. Every disappointment—even if it's tragic and evil—is *His* appointment.... He is the ultimate authority, the ultimate cause, and He has the ultimate responsibility for all that goes on.

—Kay Arthur in AS SILVER REFINED

---

6. If *God* is sovereign—then who is *not* sovereign?

> God personally knows all about tragedy. There has been no greater tragedy in history than the crucifixion of His perfect and sinless Son.
>
> —Kay Arthur in *As Silver Refined*

7. How do these verses indicate that God is no stranger to tragedy?

   a. Genesis 6:5-7

   b. Psalm 78:40-41

   c. John 3:16

8. Carefully write out **Psalm 103:19** in the space below, and begin committing this passage to memory.

In time alone with God—whose work is perfect, and who is just in all His ways (Deuteronomy 32:4)—review what you have written down and learned in this lesson. Record here any personal prayer requests that come to your heart and mind, as well as any commitments you want to express to God.

∽

BELIEVING GOD'S SOVEREIGNTY—PART 2

A companion Bible study to Chapter 8,
"Peace amid the Pain," in As Silver Refined

When tragedy and pain come our way, beloved, the only place to hide and rest secure is in the sovereignty of God....

Is this your own sure knowledge...that God is quietly working out His sovereign will in your life and in the lives of those around you?

—Kay Arthur in *AS SILVER REFINED*

---

1. What are the most significant questions that you personally have had (or have been asked by others) regarding God's sovereignty?

2. In the selections quoted in this lesson from *As Silver Refined,* underline the points that have the most personal significance for you.

> In our every painful trial, God *is* doing something about it, but often in the drama of life it's happening offstage, behind a curtain of time.
>
> —Kay Arthur in *As Silver Refined*

3. Read through the short book of Habakkuk. Use the following outline to record your understanding of what Habakkuk tells God in each section, and how God answers.

   a. 1:2-4—Summarize Habakkuk's words to God.

   b. 1:5-11—Summarize God's answer.

   c. 1:12-17 and 2:1—Summarize Habakkuk's words.

   d. 2:2-20—Summarize God's answer.

   e. 3:1-2—Summarize Habakkuk's words.

f. 3:3-15—Summarize Habakkuk's words.

g. 3:16-18—Summarize Habakkuk's closing words.

For every child of God, that's what our trials are—not a means to defeat and destroy but a way to discipline and correct. The Refiner's fire doesn't destroy; it purifies....

Whether you've got all this figured out doesn't matter. We don't have to figure it out. We don't have to understand it all. All we have to do is submit to its truth.

—Kay Arthur in AS SILVER REFINED

---

4. Express here (as thoroughly as you can) the most important lessons we can learn from the book of Habakkuk about faith, the sovereignty of God, and any other important truths that stood out to you.

God's Word doesn't say that all things are good, because
in themselves all things aren't. But God causes them all to
work together—and He keeps on causing them all to
work together—for His higher purpose, a purpose that is
infinitely good: our becoming like Jesus.

—Kay Arthur in *As Silver Refined*

5. Romans 8:28-30 is a key passage throughout Kay
   Arthur's *As Silver Refined*. Carefully look at these verses
   again.
   (a) Mark a triangle on or above every name or pronoun
   that refers to God the Father.
   (b) With a second color, mark a cross on or above every
   name or pronoun that refers to Jesus Christ.
   (c) With a third color, underline every name or
   pronoun referring to us, as believers in Christ.

ROMANS 8:28-30

And we know that God causes all things to work together
for good to those who love God, to those who are called
according to His purpose.

For whom He foreknew, He also predestined to
become conformed to the image of His Son, that He
might be the first-born among many brethren; and whom
He predestined, these He also called; and whom He
called, these He also justified; and whom He justified,
these He also glorified.

a. From what you see in these verses, how would you
   summarize God's personal love for you?

b. How would you state God's intention for your relationship with Jesus Christ, from what you see in these verses?

6. Carefully write out **Isaiah 14:24** in the space below, then begin committing this passage to memory.

In time alone with the Lord, who is our refuge and strength, review what you have written down and learned in this lesson. List here any personal prayer requests that come to your heart and mind, as well as any commitments you want to express to our loving Father.

∾

BELIEVING GOD'S SOVEREIGNTY—PART 3

A companion Bible study to Chapter 9,
"A Truth to Buy," in As Silver Refined

I know, beloved, that when you look at all the unspeakable tragedies that people must endure all this teaching about God's sovereignty can be hard to buy. But listen—and I don't mean to sound hard but only to be realistic: You either buy it or you don't. Either God is *in* control, or He's *not*. God's Word is true, or it is not true....

If it's hard for you, then simply tell that to God. Say to Him, "This is hard for me," or "I disagree with this." Then tell Him, "But I want the truth, and it's the work of your Holy Spirit to guide me into all truth." Then thank Him for the power of His Word, and receive it with meekness.

—Kay Arthur in *AS SILVER REFINED*

---

1. Summarize here the most important truths you've studied in the past two lessons about believing in God's sovereignty.

2. In the selections quoted in this lesson from *As Silver Refined,* underline the points that have the most personal significance for you.

3. Read through the first two chapters of Job. Use the following outline to record your summary of what happens in each section:

   a. Job 1:1-5

   b. 1:6-12

   c. 1:13-19

   d. 1:20-22

   e. 2:1-6

   f. 2:7-10

4. What do you believe are the most important lessons for us to learn from these chapters about God's sovereignty, and about our response to it?

5. Look also at Job's words in Job 6:8-10. From this passage, how would you describe Job's faith and character?

6. Now jump to the end of Job and read 42:1-6.

   a. What do these verses indicate about Job's trust in God's sovereignty?

   b. How do think these verses relate personally to your own trust in God's sovereignty?

7. Read also Job 42:7-17.

   a. Summarize here the final action in the book of Job.

   b. What final lessons about God's sovereignty can we draw from the book's conclusion?

> I believe with all my being that between the covers of the Bible is the answer to every situation in life.
>
> —Kay Arthur in *As Silver Refined*

8. In light of the sovereignty of God, read carefully the statements expressed in prayer to the Lord in the following verses from Psalm 119. Then restate them in your own words to our sovereign God, as an expression of your own trust and understanding of His Word.

   a. Psalm 119:15

   b. 119:30

   c. 119:45

   d. 119:50

   e. 119:64

   f. 119:66

   g. 119:75

h. 119:86-87

i. 119:91-92

j. 119:104   .

k. 119:111

l. 119:120

m.119:129

n. 119:144

o. 119:152, 160

p. 119:168

God is totally sovereign, but we don't shrug and say, "Whatever will be will be." A true understanding of the sovereignty of God (in light of all of God's Word) will not put us in a passive mode.... So on one hand is the sovereignty of God, and on the other is the accountability of man, and there's a healthy tension between the two.

—Kay Arthur in *As Silver Refined*

---

9. The book of Romans serves as an example of how the Scriptures teach together the sovereignty of God and the accountability of mankind.
   (a) In the selections from Romans printed below, mark a triangle on or above every name or pronoun representing God.
   (b) In a second color, mark the letter *S* on or above every phrase or sentence that emphasizes God's *sovereignty*.
   (c) In a third color, mark the letter *A* on or above every phrase or sentence that emphasizes every human being's *accountability* to God.

SELECTED PASSAGES FROM ROMANS

2:5-6 But because of your stubbornness and unrepentant heart you are storing up wrath for yourself in the day of wrath and revelation of the righteous judgment of God, who will render to every man according to his deeds....

3:19 Now we know that whatever the Law says, it speaks to those who are under the Law, that every mouth may be

closed, and all the world may become accountable to
God.…

9:18-21 So then He has mercy on whom He desires, and
He hardens whom He desires. You will say to me then,
"Why does He still find fault? For who resists His will?"
On the contrary, who are you, O man, who answers back
to God? The thing molded will not say to the molder,
"Why did you make me like this," will it? Or does not the
potter have a right over the clay, to make from the same
lump one vessel for honorable use, and another for
common use?

11:33,36 Oh, the depth of the riches both of the wisdom
and knowledge of God! How unsearchable are His
judgments and unfathomable His ways!… For from Him
and through Him and to Him are all things. To Him be
the glory forever. Amen.

14:10-12 For we shall all stand before the judgment seat
of God. For it is written, "As I live, says the Lord, every
knee shall bow to Me, and every tongue shall give praise
to God." So then each one of us shall give account of
himself to God.

a. From what you see in these passages, how would you
   summarize the relationship between God's
   sovereignty and man's accountability?

b. What are the most important truths these passages teach about the character of God?

Even in your weakness, you'll find that trusting in God's sovereignty will energize your testimony to others for a brighter light of witness....

Whatever your pain, people are watching. You're in this painful trial not just for your own benefit, to be made like Jesus, but also to show the world the sufficiency of Jesus Christ.

—Kay Arthur in *As Silver Refined*

---

10. For helpful review, write out **Psalm 103:19** and **Isaiah 14:24** from memory.

In time alone with the Lord, review what you have written down and learned in this lesson. Record here any personal prayer requests that come to your heart and mind, as well as any commitments you want to express to God, our loving and sovereign Father.

Finding Courage— Part I

A companion Bible study to
Chapter 10, "Strong and Courageous,"
in As Silver Refined

What is discouragement? The word is dis–courage–ment. To be discouraged is to be without courage....

We think there's no way to win in this situation. Victory looks totally unattainable.

And in truth, beloved, in that attitude and frame of heart there really is no victory—unless we deal biblically with that discouragement, unless we act on everything we've learned and thereby find the courage God freely gives.

—Kay Arthur in *As Silver Refined*

---

1. In the selections quoted in this lesson from As Silver Refined, underline the points that have the most personal significance for you.

2. Read below the opening verses in the book of Joshua.
   (a) Mark with a triangle every name or pronoun representing God.
   (b) In a second color, circle every name or pronoun representing Joshua or the people of Israel, or both.
   (c) In a third color, underline every basic *command* that

God gives to Joshua or the people of Israel.
(d) Using additional colors (if you'd like), mark a solid square block on or above every occurrence of the words *strong* and *courageous;* then place a check mark above every occurrence of the words *success* and *prosperous.*
(e) Finally, in the margin next to the passage, draw an arrow with the letter *P* above it pointing to every *promise* that God makes to Joshua or to the people.

JOSHUA 1:1-9

Now it came about after the death of Moses the servant of the Lord that the Lord spoke to Joshua the son of Nun, Moses' servant, saying, "Moses My servant is dead; now therefore arise, cross this Jordan, you and all this people, to the land which I am giving to them, to the sons of Israel. Every place on which the sole of your foot treads, I have given it to you, just as I spoke to Moses.

"From the wilderness and this Lebanon, even as far as the great river, the river Euphrates, all the land of the Hittites, and as far as the Great Sea toward the setting of the sun, will be your territory. No man will be able to stand before you all the days of your life. Just as I have been with Moses, I will be with you; I will not fail you or forsake you.

"Be strong and courageous, for you shall give this people possession of the land which I swore to their fathers to give them.

"Only be strong and very courageous; be careful to do according to all the law which Moses My servant commanded you; do not turn from it to the right or to the left, so that you may have success wherever you go.

"This book of the law shall not depart from your mouth, but you shall meditate on it day and night, so that you may be careful to do according to all that is written in it; for then you will make your way prosperous, and then you will have success.

"Have I not commanded you? Be strong and courageous! Do not tremble or be dismayed, for the LORD your God is with you wherever you go."

a. How would you summarize the most important truths this passage teaches about the character of God?

b. For you personally, what are the most motivating truths and principles you see in this passage?

God's way out of discouragement... is to simply *follow Him.*

—Kay Arthur in *AS SILVER REFINED*

---

3. In *As Silver Refined,* Kay Arthur asks, "What about you, beloved? Have you listened to the world's analysis of your condition or of your future rather than being strong and courageously believing what your God says?"
   What are the biggest contrasts you've seen between

what God says about your condition and future, and what
the world says?

Courage rather than discouragement will bring you and
me into the promises of God.

—Kay Arthur in *As Silver Refined*

---

4. Read over the ten verses of Isaiah 35 (below), which are
   words of prophecy to God's people Israel.
   (a) Circle with a bright color every word or phrase that
   relates primarily to joy.
   (b) In a second color, draw a box around every word
   relating to strength.
   (c) In another color, mark the letter *P* (for "Promise")
   over every use of the word *will.*
   (d) In another color, underline every *command* given
   here by God to His people.

ISAIAH 35:1-10

The wilderness and the desert will be glad, and the

Arabah will rejoice and blossom; like the crocus it will

blossom profusely and rejoice with rejoicing and shout of

joy. The glory of Lebanon will be given to it, the majesty

of Carmel and Sharon. They will see the glory of the

Lord, the majesty of our God.

Encourage the exhausted, and strengthen the feeble. Say to those with anxious heart, "Take courage, fear not. Behold, your God will come with vengeance; the recompense of God will come, but He will save you."

Then the eyes of the blind will be opened, and the ears of the deaf will be unstopped. Then the lame will leap like a deer, and the tongue of the dumb will shout for joy. For waters will break forth in the wilderness and streams in the Arabah. And the scorched land will become a pool, and the thirsty ground springs of water; in the haunt of jackals, its resting place, grass becomes reeds and rushes.

And a highway will be there, a roadway, and it will be called the Highway of Holiness. The unclean will not travel on it, but it will be for him who walks that way, and fools will not wander on it. No lion will be there, nor will any vicious beast go up on it; these will not be found there. But the redeemed will walk there, and the ransomed of the LORD will return, and come with joyful shouting to Zion, with everlasting joy upon their heads. They will find gladness and joy, and sorrow and sighing will flee away.

a. What are the most important lessons to learn from Isaiah 35 about courage?

b. What are the most important lessons to learn from this chapter about joy?

c. In what ways do you see any of this chapter as a picture of your own life?

5. Carefully write out **Psalm 27:14** in the space below, then begin committing this passage to memory.

In time alone with the Lord, review what you have written down and learned in this lesson. List here any personal prayer requests that come to your heart and mind, as well as any commitments you want to express to our strong and mighty God who has promised never to leave or forsake us.

FINDING COURAGE— PART 2

A companion Bible study to
Chapter 11, "A Call to Courage,"
and Chapter 12, "Where Courage Shows Most,"
in As Silver Refined

The people we admire most are those who have suffered most and yet endured with grace.... those who bear with continued suffering capture our deepest respect, and in their suffering we find ourselves drawn to the Jesus who dwells within them

—Kay Arthur in AS SILVER REFINED

---

1. In the selections quoted in this lesson from *As Silver Refined,* underline the points that have the most personal significance for you.

2. Think of someone you know who has suffered greatly "and yet endured with grace," and who manifested the presence of Christ while undergoing suffering. What observations can you make here about how this person's endurance has encouraged and ministered to you or to others?

> Perhaps more than anything else, *courage* means
> persevering... enduring... overcoming. It means
> stickability... steadfastness.
>
> —Kay Arthur in *AS SILVER REFINED*

3. The following passage follows immediately after verses
   that tell of heroic victories and miracles of deliverance.
   (a) Mark a cross over every word or phrase that tells of
   some form of trial or suffering.
   (b) Using a second color, circle every form of the word
   endure.
   (c) Using a third color, underline every positive result
   or benefit that comes to someone in this passage
   through enduring trials and suffering.
   (d) Using another color, underline words or phrases
   that tell what *we* should therefore do, in light of the
   examples in this passage.
   (e) Draw an X above any word or phrase that tells us
   what we should *not* do.

HEBREWS 11:35–12:3

...and others were tortured, not accepting their release, in
order that they might obtain a better resurrection; and
others experienced mockings and scourgings, yes, also
chains and imprisonment. They were stoned, they were
sawn in two, they were tempted, they were put to death
with the sword; they went about in sheepskins, in
goatskins, being destitute, afflicted, ill-treated (men of
whom the world was not worthy), wandering in deserts
and mountains and caves and holes in the ground.

And all these, having gained approval through their faith, did not receive what was promised, because God had provided something better for us, so that apart from us they should not be made perfect.

Therefore, since we have so great a cloud of witnesses surrounding us, let us also lay aside every encumbrance, and the sin which so easily entangles us, and let us run with endurance the race that is set before us, fixing our eyes on Jesus, the author and perfecter of faith, who for the joy set before Him endured the cross, despising the shame, and has sat down at the right hand of the throne of God. For consider Him who has endured such hostility by sinners against Himself, so that you may not grow weary and lose heart.

4. Think about the most significant challenges or trials that you believe God is asking you to endure at this time.

   a. What to you are the most difficult aspects of these challenges or trials?

   b. What have you learned in this lesson that can be most helpful for you in enduring these difficulties?

No true child of God is involuntarily a slave to any besetting sin. Sin is always a choice for the believer....

You have the power! For the true child of God, sin is simply and always a matter of choice. The power to obey is there, because the Spirit dwells within.

—Kay Arthur in *As Silver Refined*

5. Read carefully and prayerfully through Romans 6. Express here in your own grateful words your understanding of the dynamic truths in each portion of this chapter.

a. Romans 6:1-4

b. 6:5-7

c. 6:8-10

d. 6:11-14

e. 6:15-18

f. 6:19-23

6. What do you believe is the most important truth from Romans 6 that God wants you to believe and to better *live out* at this time in your life?

Be assured that when you're besieged with discouragement, *the promises of God* comprise your concentration of power, the mass of force you need to unload on the enemy.

—Kay Arthur in AS SILVER REFINED

---

7. Write below your thoughtful response to these questions from Kay Arthur:

"Do you *know* that you have an important purpose in God's plan? Do you really understand the value of *your* life? Has the significance of these words of truth sobered your thoughts so that you think as God thinks in respect to yourself? Do you realize the place you have…the purpose for your existence…the influence you wield in the way you live and in the way you redeem the hours of your day and in the relationships you form and develop? Do you understand the value and impact of your words?"

8. Summarize here the most important truths you've studied in this lesson and the last one about living in courage.

9. For helpful review, write out **Psalm 27:14** from memory.

In time alone with the Lord, review what you have written down and learned in this lesson. Record here any personal prayer requests that come to your heart and mind, as well as any commitments you want to express to our Father, the God who gives perseverance and encouragement (Romans 15:5).

Finding Joy and Hope

A companion Bible study to
Chapter 13, "Turn to the Joy of the Lord,"
and Chapter 14, "A Message of Hope,"
in As Silver Refined

Dejection is the inevitable aftermath of surrendering to discouragement. What is dejection? Dejection is lowness of spirit.... Dejection wrings you out, draining away your strength....

The secret to overcoming dejection is to put your eyes back on Jesus Christ and begin to rejoice.

—Kay Arthur in *As Silver Refined*

---

1. In the selections quoted in this lesson from *As Silver Refined*, underline the points that have the most personal significance for you.

2. Practice "putting your eyes back on Jesus Christ" by meditating on the following passages. Record your response to each one as a personal expression of praise. Notice especially any of these verses that indicate how *joy* touched the life of Christ.

   a. Matthew 11:2-6

b. Mark 1:10-11

c. Luke 10:17-20

d. Luke 10:21

e. John 15:11

f. John 17:13

g. Hebrews 12:2

3. "For help in overcoming any of the Deadly D's," writes Kay Arthur, "one of the best stories in Scripture to stay close to is that of Joseph." And she adds, "If any man had reason to become dejected, it was Joseph."

Look over the following chapters in Genesis where Joseph's story is told. For each chapter...
(a) summarize the situations Joseph was in, and how he handled them; and
(b) summarize what the chapter tells us about Joseph's relationship with God.

a. Genesis 37

b. Genesis 39

c. Genesis 40

d. Genesis 41

e. Genesis 42

f. Genesis 43

g. Genesis 44

h. Genesis 45

i. Genesis 46-47

j. Genesis 48-50

4. How would you summarize the most important lessons we can learn from the life of Joseph to help us overcome the Deadly D's?

Those who have despaired have lost or abandoned hope. They're overwhelmed with the feeling that nothing good can happen—ever again....

Despair leads to destruction.

—Kay Arthur in *As Silver Refined*

---

5. Look at the repeated questions and responses in Psalm 42:5, 42:11, and 43:5.

a. How would you express these *questions* (repeated in the first part of each verse) in your own words, to match your own times of being tempted to despair?

b. Now express the psalmist's *response* (repeated in the last part of each verse) in your own words:

I believe the greatest coup of the enemy is to cause us to *lose hope....*

When we lose hope, in essence it's because we believe that God's "lovingkindnesses" have ceased—that there's nothing more we can expect from God, that He's reached His limit....

Despair comes when you look at this moment instead of the future—because this moment can indeed be bad, this moment can indeed be evil. But our future is good, and all things now, even the evil things now, are working together to achieve it.

—Kay Arthur in *AS SILVER REFINED*

---

6. As you read the following verses from Lamentations, follow Kay Arthur's suggestion:

"Do your best to imagine yourself in this setting: The threatened captivity of God's people to Babylon had become a reality. After a prolonged siege that caused a famine so severe that parents ate their children, God had handed Jerusalem over to the enemy. He had even allowed His sanctuary to be destroyed, the magnificent temple built by Solomon with the treasures accumulated by David.

"Now Jerusalem sat desolate and lonely. The poor handful of Jews left behind lay on the ground, clothed in sackcloth and with dust on their heads. Their eyesight had faded because of their tears. Their hearts were crushed. This was affliction. This was devastation."

(a) In the first half of this passage, underline in black or gray the words or phrases that most keenly indicate the writer's pain and dejection.

(b) In the last half of the passage, circle (in the brightest color you have) the truths that are the writer's true source of hope.

LAMENTATIONS 3:13-26, 31-33

He made the arrows of His quiver to enter into my inward parts. I have become a laughingstock to all my people, their mocking song all the day. He has filled me with bitterness, He has made me drunk with wormwood.

And He has broken my teeth with gravel; He has made me cower in the dust. And my soul has been rejected from peace; I have forgotten happiness. So I say, "My strength has perished, and so has my hope from the LORD."

Remember my affliction and my wandering, the wormwood and bitterness. Surely my soul remembers and is bowed down within me.

This I recall to my mind, therefore I have hope: The LORD's lovingkindnesses indeed never cease, for His compassions never fail. They are new every morning;

great is Thy faithfulness. "The LORD is my portion," says my soul, "Therefore I have hope in Him."

The LORD is good to those who wait for Him, to the person who seeks Him. It is good that he waits silently for the salvation of the LORD....

For the Lord will not reject forever, For if He causes grief, then He will have compassion according to His abundant lovingkindness. For He does not afflict willingly, or grieve the sons of men.

a. "Therefore I have hope," we read in this passage. How would you define *hope* as it is displayed in this passage?

b. How would you summarize the most important lessons for us to learn from the big "turnaround" recorded in this passage?

Biblical hope means that what you're hoping for is something God has promised and something that will *assuredly, absolutely, unequivocally come to pass in our sovereign God's time and way*—which is always the best.

—Kay Arthur in *AS SILVER REFINED*

---

7. Carefully write out **Romans 15:13** in the space below, then begin committing this passage to memory.

In time alone with the Lord, review what you have written down and learned in this lesson. List here any personal prayer requests that come to your heart and mind, as well as any commitments you want to express to our Father, the God of hope (Romans 15:13).

∽∾

FINDING VICTORY AND RESTORATION

A companion Bible study to
Chapter 15, "Always in Triumph,"
and the conclusion, "A Fire of Reminder"
in As Silver Refined

Be assured, beloved, that the Deadly D's are *not* God's plan for your future. They are *not* Christlike, and they are *not* a part of what God is transforming you to become. The discouragement, the dejection, the despair, the demoralization—*they need never happen again to you.*

—Kay Arthur in *AS SILVER REFINED*

---

1. Look carefully at John 21. Each of the verse numbers listed below records words spoken by Jesus. All of these words were heard by Simon Peter. *Imagine that you are Peter* as you read these verses. Then, from what you know about Peter and about this situation, *record here the thoughts that might well have been going through Peter's mind* as he heard everything Jesus said.

   a. John 21:5

   b. 21:6

c. 21:10

d. 21:12

e. 21:15

f. 21:16

g. 21:17

h. 21:18

i. 21:19

j. 21:22

2. Which words of Jesus in John 21 mean the most to you personally, relative to your own life at this time?

3. In John 21, Peter received from the Lord Jesus a fresh new commission to continue following Jesus as His disciple. Jesus told Peter to feed His sheep — and in the two letters of Peter recorded in Scripture, we find him doing just that.

Read carefully over the following selections from these letters.

(a) Circle in a bright color any word that indicates joyfulness.

(b) In a second color, underline any word that indicates trial or testing.

(c) In another color, mark everything that has to do with your personal *involvement* or *relationship* with Jesus Christ, either now or in eternity.

(d) In the left margin, mark an arrow pointing to any phrase in the text that indicates the future appearing of Christ.

1 PETER 1:6-9; 4:12-13; 5:10; AND 2 PETER 3:14

In this you greatly rejoice, even though now for a little while, if necessary, you have been distressed by various trials, that the proof of your faith, being more precious than gold which is perishable, even though tested by fire, may be found to result in praise and glory and honor at the revelation of Jesus Christ; and though you have not seen Him, you love Him, and though you do not see Him now, but believe in Him, you greatly rejoice with joy inexpressible and full of glory, obtaining as the outcome of your faith the salvation of your souls....

Beloved, do not be surprised at the fiery ordeal among you, which comes upon you for your testing, as though some strange thing were happening to you; but to the degree that you share the sufferings of Christ, keep on rejoicing; so that also at the revelation of His glory, you may rejoice with exultation....

And after you have suffered for a little while, the God of all grace, who called you to His eternal glory in Christ, will Himself perfect, confirm, strengthen and establish you....

Be diligent to be found by Him in peace, spotless and blameless...

a. How would you summarize the main teaching of these passages?

b. Write a prayer to the Lord here that acknowledges the truth in these passages, and how it relates to your own life.

4. Look over the previous twelve lessons.

   a. Restate here (in summary form) the most important truths you have studied personally in this book.

b. What do you believe are the most important changes God wants to see in your life as a result of your study in this book?

5. For helpful review, write out **Romans 15:13** from memory.

In time alone with God, review what you have written down and learned in this lesson. List here any personal prayer requests that come to your heart and mind, as well as any commitments you want to express to God, our gracious and forgiving Father.